A WALK ON SNOW

Poems and reflections of an African immigrant to Winter Land.

Patrick Mpulubusi

(mpulubusi.patrick@gmail.com)

Dedication

To my wife Kathleen:

I believe I am still alive because of you. I love you.

To my children Sarah, Jay & Nellie: My love for you is in your blood. I hope you feel it every day. Sarah you inspired me to publish my poetry.

To Don Delaney (my mulamu) or my brother-in-law: You are a blessing. Your support cannot be measured.

To my late sisters, Carol and Patricia: Your spirits live on with me. I have had a chat with you both since you have been gone to the shadows. Thank you for your support. Sisters-in-law FOREVER.

To Ray Garford: I could call you Sekuru (uncle) or brother, but thank you for being a true friend of mine.

To my relatives in Zambia: I miss you.

To my friends in Canada: Thank you for your friendship and support

Table of contents

A Snowy Welcome

the first day i left africa i felt uplifted to the sky.

the first day i walked on canadian snow
i slipped and fell.

i arrived in edmonton in winter. snow was falling.

i thought then it was a heavy cloud
crumbling and falling and pilling on
the ground.

this was snow. it was cold.

it was frozen moisture.

after the fall i had to rise.

i have never risen from ice because i
had never fallen on ice.

i had lived on solid ground all my life. i
had the courage to uplift myself out of
africa. but i lost the courage to uplift
myself from the cold ice.

i lay there on cold ice, heartbroken and frozen.

my lofty expectations of a beautiful country
froze and shattered.

rise and flee now said a cold voice. go
back to africa.

Introduction.

my name is john lusumpuko if i charged a dollar for the question that follows my pronouncement of my name, i would be a rich person by now. “how do you say your last name?”

“lu (loo) us (so) mpuko.”

“could you say that again a little slower?”

“lu- (loo) -su (soo)- mpu (mpuu)- ko (koh).”

“that is hard to say. the “m” is silent. i can’t say your name. can i just call you by your first name, john?”

“sure, no problem. i don’t mind at all. i feel much more comfortable if you called me john. i am afraid the harder you try to pronounce my last name, the closer you are to saying a swear word!”

my last name became the first stumbling block to my new life in this new country. the white immigration officer at the airport could not pronounce my last name. many more people, not only white canadians, could not say my african name. i believe i missed many employment opportunities because of my last name.

when i migrated to a canada, i had to survive the shock of uprooting myself from my country in africa. just like transplanting a tree, i had to undergo the shock of being transplanted into the new land. before the tree takes roots, the leaves wilt or fall off and die. the tree may die completely. for the tree to survive it needs a lot of water and good nutrients. it needs support so the wind doesn't blow it down. if it survives the initial shock, it may not produce fruit in the beginning. for the tree to survive and grow and produce fruit, it needs a lot of care from all sources. it has to assimilate to the soils, to the climate, to the amount of sunshine it receives in a year and the surrounding vegetation.

humans need to assimilate to the language, new culture, beliefs, sometimes religion, behaviors, ethics and the climate of the new country. this acclimatization and assimilation will only succeed if the people of the land open up and allow for the process to take place.

my choice to migrate, leave homeland in africa, uproot my life, did not have a well thought survival plan in the new land. cutting myself off from the ancestral land and from the clan, leaving sunshine and pure air and shame cooked in a black pot on wood fire, triggered a shock wave in my life.

i had difficulty in adjusting to the snow. i spent the mornings watching the snow piling up on the roads and the roofs across the street. i wondered if the roofs were going to collapse from the weight of the falling snow. i wrote this poem:

snow

that fluffy mist

falls silently from crumbling clouds.

snow

makes a soft landing on the ground with cold feet and cold feel.

snow lands and waits in cold white piles of fluff

till the hot sun and warm wind comes along to blow it away.

i would see a person dressed in heavy clothes, from head to the feet, face and hands all covered up walking in the deep snow. i would wait for the sun to rise from the east. on a snowy day the sun never rose.

i did dress up in heavy clothes a few times and ventured into the snow. with winter boots laced up, i would take a walk around the block. walking on snow felt like walking on sand. fresh snow shifted under the boots. it gave no real traction. i learned the hard way that some parts of the sidewalk were very slippery. frozen ice was covered by fresh snow. one day while taking a walk, i stepped onto that frozen ice below the fresh snow. i slipped and fell, hard. my feet went in opposite directions. i felt like i split the skin between my legs. i landed on the sidewalk with my feet 180 degrees apart. that really hurt. it took me a good five minutes before i could get up.

some days while taking a walk in the snow i would take off my gloves and scoop the snow and play with it in my hands. it felt cold to touch. as the snow falls on you it does not stick to your clothes. you can dust it off with your hand just like regular dust. when you step into a big pile of snow, some of it goes into your boots and melts and makes your socks wet.

one day i am walking around the block. i meet an old white man. he looks at me and he notices i am a black person. at the time i was the only black person who lived in that neighborhood. he stopped to greet and ask me where i was from. when i told him i was from africa, he laughed at me and further queried me why i left africa to come to this miserable weather. i did not answer his question truthfully. i told him i was a student at the university. the scholarship required me to study here. he wished me "good luck with weather" with a hidden grin. he shook his completely covered head and continued his walk.

as days and weeks passed, i ventured into the malls by taking the bus. most of the time, i would be the only black person on the bus. the few people who were brave enough to approach me would ask me where i was from. when i told them i was from africa, some laughed at me, some showed concern if i would survive the cold weather of edmonton.

eventually spring arrived, melting away the piles and hills of snow. i could feel my frozen body melting slowly. the sun warmed up the outside air, considerably. i would see more people walking about in the streets. i saw grass and dry leaves that had been covered by layers of snow for the first time. that was my first spring and i sprung to life.

Summer does come to Edmonton.

once the winter and spring wind is
gone by
to the end of the south pole the
warm wind blows inward.
warm smiles follow.

the sun shines with
confidence rays of hope from
the sun bring out the bloom
of beautiful flowers and bees.

children pour out into the park
with shrieks and laughter
to welcome the abundant
warmth and bloom of the land

finally, i am freed from
the depressing

gloom and doom of the cold winter. i am staying here for summer.

the sun rose earlier in the morning. the sun brought warmth. the sun brought bright light. the sun stayed up much longer. the sun brought gentle showers of rain. the sun brought thunder. the sun brought a warm smile to my life. leaves on trees and the grass on the ground grew green. flowers bloomed in the gardens. more people got out and walked

about in the streets without coats on. the sun of spring brought all frozen things back to life. i felt alive. i became alive. summer came. the river valley grew green. the warmth and the greenery of the city brought the feel of my home in africa.

unfortunately, within a few months, summer came to an end. i wrote this poem:

at the end of summer dead leaves
and flowers hang in the wind in
flight.

a song of love and beauty
written on the crumpled petals is
blown away to summer's end.

the grass and the bushes are smothered by fallen leaves and dying foliage. birds perch no more on the empty branches. in droves, they fly high above in the sky in flight to the south in search of another summer, for the prairie summer is over
for me, a cold breeze, the cooling sun, discourages me from taking my evening stroll down the street. a hint of snow in the air tells me to

get ready for a long cold
winter season.
i was now rooted in the ground.

when winter arrived for another
season, i was ready for it. i slowly
saw my roots regenerating into the
deep snow and past permafrost of
my new land. i overcame the
shock of the transplantation.

my wilted spirit and my frozen
heart slowly defrosted because of the
warm light that came from the
hearts of many people of this new
land.

white and none white people, i
slowly got to know, helped untie
the knot that was strangling me.
loneliness, homesickness,
joblessness and lack of personal
confidence had me by the throat.

my new roots are now permanently established here. i have no words in my mouth. i don't have words good enough to convey the beam of love and gratitude to all the people who saved me from freezing completely. thank you very much to all of you. keep the warmth flowing into winter land.

Make my day.

when the sun came back to winter
land
a burst of warm joy filled my
cold heart.
the wind accompanying the
sun blew the cold away

to the north in a hurry.
the snow man hiding in my
chest melted away
his cold fangs lost the grip to
my soul.
the darkness and clouds
disappeared into the forest.

the moon was up there with a
smile and with no purpose
and the stars dimmed
and disappeared.

i thanked the sun for the warmth
and the warm smile it brought to
my life.
the warm sun made my day.

Things to do before departure.

i knew before hand; i was migrating to the land of white people. my mother told me to be clean. cleanliness is next to godliness. the white pastor at the local church, many years ago, emphasized that to my mother. i was made to believe that white people were as white as god, inside and outside.

all the days before my departure, i cleaned myself. took two baths every day. shaved my facial hair every day. physical cleanliness transformed my appearance. my clan members believed i was turning white.

before i could be certified clean to enter canada the doctor ordered for my blood. the blood had to be clean. my blood was examined for viruses and parasites and bacteria. every blood cell was examined microscopically. after two months i received a letter. my blood was found clean and good to enter canada.

the final step: morality cleanliness. i was required to provide official proof from the police and the courts of the land to show that i was not a thief or murderer or rapist or just a thug. i was cleared of all these immoralities. joy and happiness overflowed in me.

i then convinced myself to take one personal step further. i needed to upgrade my spoken english to a nasal sound. and my skin had to be

polished with some whitish
powder and some cream.

i had to polish my teeth to a sparkling
white. i had to clean my breath. no
fish. no garlic, no curry in my diet.
only white bread and white rice.
drank clear water and milk. to
complete the transformation, i
married a white woman.
i entered canada with excitement
and great expectation.

i believed and convinced myself that
the people of this new land had to be
heavenly clean physically and
morally. time proved me wrong.

i landed in canada in midwinter.
the land was white. everything was
white.

but... this was winter land full
of snow with icy roads and
frozen rivers.

my personal spirit could not take it.
i was abandoned by my spirit. my
dream froze.
i began my life on a slippery road.

Just return the love.

before leaving home land the
clan advised me:
take a sharp knife. you have to
carve out your mother's heart. take
it with you. you will need it if you
are to succeed in this long journey.
keep your mother's heart safe and
secure it in your chest. it is full of
love and spiritual powers.

when you arrive at your new
destination, if your mother's heart
does not break along the way,
wrap it in a golden box and send it
back home.

more advice:
take your birth spirit with you. most
important, the night before departure
spend a night at the clan's

graveyard. convince your birth spirit to go with you. you will need it for your spiritual guidance and protection in that new unfamiliar place.

New to the land.

when i landed in canada i was told:
you have never been here. no one
from your clan has ever set foot on
this land. there is no foot print here
on this land that belongs to your
clan. no shadow of your mother
ever stood here.

you landed here unannounced.
no one is here to open the gates for
you. no one is here to guide you. you
have no protector in this land. you
are truly marooned. you are now a
slave.

the chief of this new land will set you
free after you have served your time.
it has been many years since i
arrived here in canada. i am still

serving my time in a minimum wage paying job.

Choices in life

if life is hard work, choose
hard work.
if learning is hard work, choose
hard work.
if education is hard work, choose
hard work.
if getting rich is hard work,
choose hard work.
if making friends is hard
work, choose hard work.

if finding happiness is hard work,
choose hard work.
if you don't choose hard work
then, hunger, failure,
homelessness, mental depression
and death will find a friend in you.

Do not doubt yourself.

you don’t have to look up for the
sun in the sky to acknowledge day
time. you don’t have to squeeze your
pressure points
to prove you have a heartbeat.
believe in yourself.

I am lost.

i am here. i want to discover myself. first, i should explore my ignorance. i don't know when the sun was created. was it the first thing that showed up in the universe? no one knows the answer. this is a collective ignorance for humanity.

the sun shines whenever it shows up in the sky. this has been going for unknown number of years. the sun has infinite source of power.

whenever the sun is shining in the sky, i want to look at it. i can't ask the sun to look at me. i love the feel i get from the sun. i do ask many questions when cold clouds block the sun; when is the sun going to show up today? where is the sun today? is it true the sun is smaller than the stars? if that is true why do stars wait for the sun to disappear for them to show up?

the little flying bats don't like the sun. they go to sleep when the sun is shining. why?

if the sun loses its power to shine the forests will die. there will be no rainfall. the oceans and rivers will freeze over. the wind stops blowing. the air that we breathe becomes contaminated because the leaves that purify it are dead. everyone has to buy an oxygen tank. we have to depend on manufactured foods and melted ice water. by now we are dependent on nuclear electric power stations. hydroelectric stations are frozen over. eventually nuclear power stations run out of water and coolants.

boom...there is the answer.
nuclear armageddon.
but i don't believe this scenario.
there was no beginning of the sun
and there is no ending of the sun.

Confronting myself.

lost. my senses are lost.
i am feeling lost.
i know i am not lost.
i chose to be here. it was my
choosing to be here.

still i am lost. my senses cannot
register my whereabouts. it is a
strange place.
it is a new place.
my brain has gone into a
slow motion.

the process of verifying this new
environment has taken all the brain
resources. i have a feeling, by now, it
will take a while to capture and store
all the details.
i don't know. i have no
knowledge about this world.

but i am here. i ask myself many
questions.
i want to know how this world came
to being.

this world is strange to me. how
was it created. where did the first
rock come from? where did the first
molecule come from? was there a
someone responsible for the
creation of this world?
where did this being come from?
how did life begin from nothing?
could creation have started from
nothing? that is not possible.

but i stand here on solid rock.
i swim in vast oceans.
i see the sun and the moon and
the stars.
i see elephants and lions and zebras
and buffaloes.
i see birds flying across the sky.

these things i see are true evidence
of creation. the things i see are proof
of creation. maybe they are also
proof of the existence of the creator.

i am still lost. i am still ignorant.
how did it all begin?
how will it all end? all i know i will
not be here when the end comes.
i should just be happy to be here to
witness the existence of this
universe. i am just happy to be
part of this amazing universe!

No fear.

i fear not death
but what shall be the bearer of my
death:
a boulder rolling off the mountain.
thunderbolt from the sky.
drowning. swept away by a raging
river.

mauled by a hungry lion in the
green forest.
death on the highway struck by a
fast truck.
death on the street corner
struck by a cop's bullet.

death in my bed
eaten away by cancer.
surely;
am not afraid of death
i fear the bearer of death.

Hope.

the sun is gone down west
to fetch out our tomorrow.
the sun is gone down west
to let out the stars and the moon.
the sun is gone down west
to let the night bring us
sweet dreams
and brighter tomorrow.

Find your direction

when i am lost in my life journey
i don't look for road signs to find
my right direction.
i follow the trail of my life's
trash. there is a sign along the
way covered with my life's trash.
that is the road sign i missed.

Inspiration.

when the wind is silent
and the sun gone to sleep
i hear the whisper of stars
in the dark of my mind.
when the clouds are rolled away
the sun and the moon and the
stars shine my path to wisdom.

Honor thy father

my father dispensed his
wisdom with a strap and a stick
at times he forgot to load the strap
with wisdom
but with hurt and pain.
my love and honor for him
healed my memory scars.

Self-confidence.

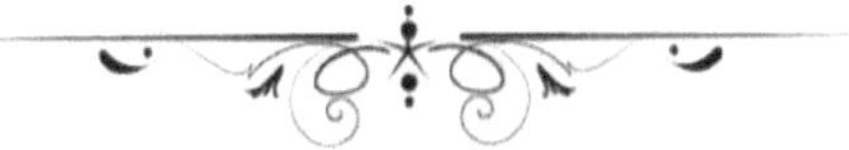

when thunderstorm is roaring and dark clouds are approaching and the ferocious wind is blowing hard, the mountain stands its ground. you are the mountain.

Mystery of creation

where there is no beginning
there is no ending.
if there is a beginning
there is an ending.
if there was a beginning of this
universe,
then what was there before the
beginning?

if there was nothing, then the
beginning began from nothing!
imagine nothingness turning into
something as large as the universe!

my mind frequently travels back
from this universe to its
beginnings. when my mind reaches
the imaginary beginning point, it
freezes and shuts down.

Mother nature is not to blame.

if you chose to climb a tall tree to
the highest branch and the branch
broke, and you fell to the ground
and broke your bones. who is to
blame?

•••

if you chose to climb the tallest
mountain and you slipped off the
cliff and fell into the gorge below
and most likely you died. who is
to blame?

•••

if a fierce hurricane came from the
sea and roared into the land and
blew away the house you built by the
sea shore. who is to blame?

•••

gravity is the loving hand mother
nature uses to hold on to us so that
we are not swept away to the moon.

•••

mother nature lives in the high
mountains to keep an eye over us.
it is forbidden to climb to this
sacred space.

•••

when mother nature has to clean
up the sea and the atmosphere, she
sends out her crew named
hurricane, monsoon, typhoon and
tornado.

•••

Bridges in your life.

you have a long-life journey
ahead. there are many bridges to
cross. on your journey
there will be broken bridges,
there will be collapsed bridges,
there will be bridges under
construction,
there will be washed away bridges.

to complete the life journey
you need to carry a bag full of
luck, life skills
and tools for life.

Mother love.

my mother's womb
my sweet home
my first home
my life began in there
my home built of love
my home built with care
and wisdom of the old.

and filled with laughter.
i drank love from your umbilical cord.
i ate my first meal from your breast.
now i am grown.

not too old to drink more love from your cup.
i need more love and wisdom
i want to share it with my children
and my friends
and the world.

your love is sweeter and better.

it will make the world better.

Racist outlook

thought of creation:
imagine creation.
if everything created was painted
in one color.

what a hopeless, boring earth
that would be.
take a look in the garden of flowers
and smell the precious gift of colors.

Believe in equality.

when you accept the life you are given, understand that it is finite. it is your responsibility to sustain it to its finite cycle.

tap into the wisdom inherent in you to defend yourself and others who are created with different sets of abilities. it is inherent in you to love other beings whether black or white or yellow or brown.

we are not just born. we are created. all of us human creatures are created equal. we have to love one another.

Eyes for racial divide.

as a new immigrant
i loved taking my children to the
playground where other parents
gathered with their children. mainly
in playgrounds in the neighborhood.

whenever i brought my
brown children to play
i had to listen with my eyes. i
would see sideways glances,
a sudden hand pulling a child to
the side.

a whisper passed to their child. the
child turning away from my brown
child at play.
i saw hovering around their child.

i saw visible discomfort in my
presence.

i saw the unspoken message. you are
not welcome here.
i suffered the pain for my children.
they had no idea of the racial divide.

Bi-lingual: English and mother tongue

i am not fluent in canadian english. i spoke my birth language very well as a child.
speaking in my mother tongue,
words come through easily.
words form on my tongue and
roll out a clear speech.

while i was in my mother's belly my
ears picked up and stored words
spoken by mother. i also spoke my
mother tongue while growing up.

years after my birth i had to
learn english words.
my word storage was literary full by
then. there was not enough word
storage left.

english words had to be
accommodated. but when english
language became mandatory form of
communication in the land,
i had to make room for english
words in the word storage. i had to
delete words my mother installed.

now that the two languages are
imbedded on my tongue the
two languages are fighting for
dominance.

when i want to speak, my lips and
my tongue have trouble getting out
the words in the desired language.
there. now you understand. there
is a war of words raging on my lips.

i speak with an accent. because
my tongue is at war for words.
i speak harmonized english. the
people here call it an accent.

The heart will rejoice.

lessons learned in childhood.
walking. one step at a time.
stumble, stumble and fall.
stumble, stumble and make a step.

step, step and stand, stand, walk
and walk.
stand and walk. walk. away, walk
away.
from bad environment. from
bad friendships.
from bad love relationships. from
bad habits.
from bad employers.

stop!

look and see. identify the right
direction.

when your feet arrive in the
right place
the heart will dance. thy soul
shall rejoice.

Time is thy enemy.

time!
where has time gone? people always ask.
take a mirror and look at yourself.
look for time in your reflection.
if you are bald your hair absorbed time and dissolved. if you have a head full of white hair time is hiding in there.

look for time in your face. see those wrinkles, time is hiding in those ridges and furrows. time makes you look old and wrinkled. look at your chin. if it is sagging time is hidden in that fat sac.

you can find time hidden in parts of your body. in your breast. in your large belly. in your large thighs.

if your joints hurt time is hiding in
there. if you can no longer walk fast
time is slowing you down.

time is not on your side. time will
eventually stop you cold. if you are
one of those people who say you
are wasting my time. the fact is
time is wasting you away instead.
time does not slow down to save you.
but you will be wasted by time.

Pain of losing a friend.

i did not get the memo of your date
of departure from our common
ground to the underground home
of the buried. my heart grieves
every day. my soul is drained out.

there are vases of flower bouquets
on your grave. i am kneeling. and
others are kneeling before wilted
flowers.

ribbons of sorrow bind our hearts
together in grief. we are here
clasping and gripping to the false
hope of seeing you again.

time has not healed the pain. time
has not cleared away our memories.
i miss you my dear friend. we miss
you.

The one I love.

long time ago. many sunsets ago. my
mother the only one who had me in
her soft belly spoke to me in my
mother tongue.
she said one day in the future, after
many moons, when you are grown
up, you shall meet the one who
loves you. and that is the one you
will love.

at first, she will be a stranger to
you. and you will be a stranger to
her. when you meet, her heart will
smile at you. your heart will smile
back at her.

you will ask her to sit beside you. she
will sit with you on the moon's
shadow. you will count stars in the

sky together. you will both smile
at the lovers' ghost as it passes by.

you will hear the echo of silent
music in the wind. your hearts
shall dance to the rhythm of silent
love music. forever together.

A view from the top of the mountain.

there are mountains here.
mountains of the world. i read books
about these canadian rocky
mountains. african schools taught
about these mountains.

when i came to canada curiosity
drove me to one of the peaks of
the mountains.
from the peak i could see as far as
the sky meets the mountain range.
even in the midsummer heat, the
top of the mountain was covered in
snow and ice. i saw water from
melting ice cascading through the
crevices.

lakes filled with blue water stretched
between. the beauty of the
mountains lay in the distant view.

but where i stood, lay loose rock
and boulders on the verge of rolling
down the steep mountain into the
deep valley below. i felt little
mountain tremors. i realized then
that creation was not yet complete.

The shadow.

the shadow is visible but
not touchable.
always silent. always with me
sometimes startling.

disappears in the darkness.
always on the opposite side of light.
the dark side of me.

Sweet home.

a home is a place of comfort. families or friends are bonded by the comfort of the place. the bonding agents are truth, love, trust and joy. these are four pillars of a home.

members of the home can leave the place at some point. in time, everyone returns, in a day or in a week or in a month or in years.

everyone tells their story about the adventure of their time away. if everyone tells the truth the bonds are strengthened. if lies are told the bonds will weaken. the home foundation weakens and breaks up. love, trust and joy rot away. everyone scatters.

The home I grew up in.

it was a little mud house with a
cone shaped roof thatched with
brown grass.
my father built it out of love
and poverty.
in this little mud house, my
mother cooked shame from
pounded corn. shame was shared
among children and passersby.

in this little mud house mice and
lizards and bats hid in the walls.
in this little mud house, my brother
was born. my sister was born.

in this little mud house, the dog
stole the shame from the clay pot.
in this little mud house grandma
told us stories of the past.

in this little mud house family
memories are stuck to the smoke-
stained walls. my childhood
shadows linger forever. sweet
home.

Grow out of poverty.

from dark to grey to orange the horizon in the east changes over the hills. the sun rises casting shadows of sadness in my morning dreams. the grey mist hovers above. the first rays of the morning sun shoot through holes in the walls of my hut.

in my dream, i wakeup. my feet are cold. i am hungry. i have not eaten for days. i need food for strength. i look around. i find scattered grains dropped by birds and mice. i roast them over a little fire. i eat the grains. a little strength fills my weak muscles.

a song of hope forms on my blistered lips. my dream continues.

i see a smiling cloud hovering in
my open door. it beckons me to
follow. i get up and follow it
through a narrow-ragged path.

the path is flanked by thorny bushes
and dew laden grass that swipe at my
eyes. i hear hissing snakes and
howling hyenas and i get scared.

but the guiding cloud keeps my
hope unbroken. painfully i follow
the cloud on the steep hills. the
cloud tells me to take a rest. i sit on
one of the rocks.

in a gentle voice the cloud
commands me to gaze and i gaze at
the land below.
i see a large glittering river flowing
gracefully across tribal lands.
fish jumping in and out of the clear
water.

i see virgin land sprawling to the
end of my vision.
i see buffalos and gazelles and
antelopes grazing the waltzing green
grass.

why do you starve in this land
which has rich soils and wild life?
why do you die of thirst when clean
water is flowing away in
abundance. why don't you bathe
your body stench in that river? the
cloud asks me in a gentle voice.
the cloud vanishes in the mist.
i descended the hills at a
breaking speed. i jumped into the
river. i swam. i drank the water. i
caught fish.

i was on my way to my hut with my
fish.
from the bushes, men in
green uniforms with guns and
dogs appeared.

i was arrested and charged
with trespassing
and illegal fishing in a privately-owned land. the land was owned by a rich corrupt politician. i was taken to jail.

the dream was interrupted by buzzing flies and birds and mice. i was hungry that morning. i had not eaten a meal in days.

i woke up. i sat up. the dream was still very vivid in my mind. it felt real. i attended a political rally a few days earlier. the message i got from the rally was clear. the speaker was the politician in the dream. his message:

we waged a gallant war against the colonial oppressors. it was a vicious battle and we won. victory and

freedom are our new songs written
in blood forever in your heart.

our new frontier is to combat
poverty hunger, disease and
illiteracy. this is the promise that i
will dedicate my life to. that was
the promise that stuck to my heart.

the irony of this promise was that
it was delivered in the colonial
master's language
with an interpreter for the
local masses.
the politician wore an expensive
suit made by the colonial masters.

he wore dark sun glasses to protect
his eyes from the African sun.
that is the man who owns the rich
land in the valley.
this has been our ancestral land
since the beginning of time. no one
is allowed to hunt in that land

anymore.many years of independence. many years since the promise. yet the people are starving in this valley. i am starving. i am no longer allowed to fish or hunt in my ancestral land. it is time to fight another war. this time against my new corrupt leaders.

The disturbing dream.

my mother held her chest with
her two hands
her two powerful hands lifted
her two breasts to the sky.
there is no milk left in them
she cried out loudly
i am not able to feed you and
your siblings anymore.

you are at the age of a hunter and
warrior.
here my son.
touch my breast.
take the spirit from my breast. it
is the spirit of your forefathers.

i bestow it upon you. you are now of
age. you are the one. you are the
one to provide and defend the
family and the clan and our land.

go into the valley and hunt for food.
there is a lion out there. there is a
leopard. there are men in green
uniforms with dogs in the valley.
you have to defend yourself. take the
family spear. it has the protective
power of our ancestors.
this is our land. this land of ours
has provided and protected us from
unknown time to now. no one shall
take it away from the clan. go my
son. go into the valley. go hunt.

anyone who dare stop you or
arrest you shall face the wrath of
our ancestors.
i was hungry and i was angry. i was
armed. no one dared stop me. i went
hunting. the forest was bountiful.
the hunt was a success.

Courage and determination.

fear is the loss of courage. when you are herding cattle in the forest you don't want to hear the lions roar. courage melts away from your entire body. fear grips you.
when you facing adversity, grip your courage and raise your clenched fist.

Careful who you talk to.

you should guard your pillow with
all your wits.
why?
because it is filled with all your
dreams, your sorrows and your
love secrets.

Inner pain and sorrow.

pain is the bullet that pierces the
heart.
sorrow is the poison that corrodes
away the soul and numbs the mind.

Happiness and hatred

you have to work hard to invite bliss, happiness and joy into your home. but hatred and hurt are the frequent passersby near your home.

Healing sea waves. my dream.

i am laying down on the beach by the blue ocean waters. the ocean god riding on a grand roaring wave commands me to go for a ride on this giant wave. at the command i rise. i take a big step into the sea.

a giant wave picks me up. with no fear i grasp at the sails of the wind. the giant wave powered by the great wind takes me away over the ocean to the blue mountain on the far island. far as the eye can see. and went past the blue mountain towards the beautiful sunset.

in the radiant orange sunset, in the calm winds, the ocean god opens my heart with gracious hands. a deep orange light gushes into my whole body. my body, my heart, my mind and my soul are cleansed and healed.

when i awake on the white sand beach, i feel relaxed and i am wrapped in a sea wave of happiness. i love the beach.

Cure for winter blues.

i suffer from that seasonal affective disorder (sad). every winter i suffer from a mild depression caused by lack of sunshine. the sun provides vitamin d.

i am african. vitamin d from the sun was available 12 months a year. in canada winter or the cold season goes on for up to seven months. in those months, the sun is sometimes covered by clouds. sunny winter days are cold.

i can't go outside. i spend my days indoors. being indoors and lack of vitaminD from the sun triggers a mental depression. vitaminD from the pharmacy does help me survive the winter blues, but barely.

the nagging questions people ask me is: why did you come here? why did you leave sunshine africa? did you not do some simple research on canadian weather before migrating? why can't you just go back to africa?
... ok. enough. i get it...
my way of curing sad is as follows: i would like to ask a doctor to open my chest to let out all that cold air i feel inside me. then fill up my veins with warm milk full of vitamin d.

then open my skull and clean up all cold thoughts that come with mental depression or trigger it. then shine a beam of sunshine on the dark spots of my brain caused by lack of vitamin d. then heat up all the cold brain cells with a sun beam. that should cure my sad. drastic, eh.

taking a vacation in the tropic
works much better than anything
else. escape winter land to the
sunny beaches.
lessons learned: when winter
arrives,
just escape the winter. go to the
warm tropics.

Bitten by frozen air.

i don't have the word in my mother
language to explain frost bite to my
mother. i wanted to let my mother
know i had frostbite to my ears. i
could interpret this by saying i had
my ears bitten off by the cold wind.

i had frostbite. my ears were
bleeding. the bite was painful. i
cried frozen tears.

my mother responded: the wind
does not bite. no one has ever been
bitten by cold wind over here in
africa.

i could not argue with my mother.
i had no words to explain frostbite.
so, i have learned to dress for the
winter season.

bundle up. cover up. dress up for
winter.
be careful. winter has a painful
cold bite. on your skin and in your
soul and mind.

Remembering sorrow.

i was a young boy then, at the
funeral of my cousin. dead. taken
away from this earth. i was maybe
ten. it was my first time to witness
death of a human being. funeral. it
was a gathering. i can't forget it.

i saw all faces of the young and
elderly. long sad drooping faces.
death weighed on everyone to
the ground. every eye gushing
out a flood of tears.

only grandma, with her shriveled
hand reached out. she touched the
lifeless body. everyone. all of us at
that moment whispered a silent
prayer and goodbye.

death reigned that day. death hurt.
i can't forget.

Mother's tears.

when my brother died my mother
wept. tears of pain rained.
when my next brother passed on my
mother mourned in songs of
sorrow. and when my other brother
was taken away out of this earth my
mother was stricken by severe grief.

her stricken body and soul were
shattered and crumbled to dust.
she was almost gone out of this
world. as she lay down on the bare
soil grandma poured a bucket of
water over her crumbled body. it
was the shower of life. her life
returned. over time she
blossomed into an everlasting
flower. my mother is still smiling
in her advanced age.

Grandma 's and Grandpa's

my grandpa lived for, an estimated, 104 years. he spent his last years under mango trees he planted. the trees were very tall and shady. he had a comfortable chair my father bought for him. every morning during the dry season grandpa would take his chair and place it under the shade of a mango tree. he also had a little wooden table where his food and cup of water was served. his bible was always on the table. he sat on the chair the whole day unless he had to go to the toilet to relieve himself.

he was among the first people who had learned to read when the white settlers colonized the region. he was also among the first people to be

converted to christianity by white missionaries.
in his last years of life, he mainly read the bible and other literature from the local church run by white missionaries. whenever i visited my grandparents, he would read the bible to me. he also liked taking long naps between his meals.

here is my poem i wrote for grandpa:
grandpa do not slumber in that cozy chair of yours. wake up and talk to me.
i want the words of wisdom you have accumulated. i want to inherit them.

grandpa wake up. tell me: how many thunderstorms did you survive in your life time? how many rainbows did you count in your life time? and where did they disappear to? how did you survive all these decades?

what is the secret to long life? how
many strangers did you feed and
shelter under your roof?

grandpa wake up. do not let the
thought of your end of life sadden
your soul. i need to hear the
wisdom before it is buried with you.
yes. i hear your mumbles: love and
kindness and respect for your
fellow man is the secret to long life.
thank you, grand pa.

For my grandma:

a little mud house stands under a
giant mango tree.
smoke always smolders from the
roof.
chickens and dogs go in and out of
the small house.
a cat covered in ashes purrs by
the fireside.
black flies zoom in and out of
the house. some sit on the wall.

little grandchildren run in and out
of the little house all day.
grandma cooks nshima and okra from
the little house. grandma keeps a long
stick. she walks with it all day.

quiet often she swings her long
stick. once in a while lands it good
on a chicken or on a dog or on her

grandchild or on the cat. but her swing is too slow for the fly.

First time going to city.

i cried with excitement when my father agreed to take me to the city for the first time. the city was many kilometers away from our village. we had to catch a ride on the back of a lorry five kilometers from our village. i was about twelve years old then. i hardly slept the night before.

i woke up before anyone stirred that morning. i put on my clean clothes my mother had washed and ironed the day before. around six in the morning my father and i walked to the lorry station. the gravel road was very bumpy and dusty. it took us two hours to reach the city. my clean clothes were covered in dust. so was everyone in the back of the lorry.

the city was exciting. it was fascinating to see so many vehicles. there was honking, sirens blurring, loudspeakers and tall buildings. crowds of people in the streets. i was overwhelmed. i was getting dizzy from watching out for vehicles and motor cycles, bikes and people in a hurry.

we finally got to a shop that sold food and soft drinks.

i was hungry. we did not have breakfast before we left home. my father bought me a bottle of fanta and a bun. this was the best food. everyone who ever went to the city talked about drinking fanta orange. once in a while dad would buy the drink and bring it home for my mother.

she would then share it with me and my siblings. but today i got the whole bottle of fanta and bun to myself. i was a very happy child. we

went outside of the shop and i leaned on the wall to enjoy my special meal.
i did not expect beggars in the city. dirty people walking barefoot with an overpowering body stench. as i was eating and drinking my special meal, one of these beggars approached us. he stood close to me and said to my father: elder man i am very hungry. i have no job. i have no money to buy food. i have no home. life in the city streets is rough and tough. i have not eaten anything for the last two days.

his teeth had a greenish coating layer. his breath and body odors were stronger than the sewer smell. i could not continue eating my food. before my father could say anything, i handed over my fanta and my bun to the man. as he was saying thank you to me, i took a few steps to the side of the store and vomited. when i was done puking my father led me away. he promised to buy me more food later.

we walked to the main street in a hurry. as we waited for the traffic light to turn green, i looked to my left. i saw a few more beggars standing there with hands stretched out:

beggars, not hurried but worried
walking the street with sad faces
to nowhere.
some mumbling and shuffling
along the street
with a hand stretched in hopeless
despair.

when we crossed the main street to the shops on the other side, there was a woman who was completely blind. i was amazed to see a blind person. at my age of twelve i had never seen a blind person. she had no eyeballs. i could see hollow spaces where eyeballs used to be. she was with a little girl covered in dust, bare foot and ad a shredded dress on.

the girl called out to us as we passed by: could you please help us with money for food? my father was touched by the girl's plea. we stopped. my father fished out coins from his pocket and handed them to the girl. she claps and then cups both her hands to receive the coins from my father. she utters words of thanks in a voice that evokes pity in my stomach.

we leave the woman and her the child and head to the supermarket.

on the corner of the supermarket
we find a beggar who has no legs. he
is sitting on his bum.

when i see him, i am gripped
with fear? another first.
i had never seen a person who is like
that. i had never seen a human
being who had no legs at all.

he moved using his hands.
he plants his hands on the
pavement and raise his torso and
moves it forward.
i am truly afraid of this man. i
am nervous as we go past the
man. i walk fast as we pass him.

i don't have the courage to take
glance at the man even after we have
gone past a few meters.
my father does not seem to be
disturbed or concerned at all.

he noticed that i was nervous and afraid. he tells me has seen this man in the street for many years. whenever he comes to the city, he sees this man on the same location. he informs me he has given money to the man in the past.

he tells me that there are rumors that the man owns a big house in the townships and also owns a grocery shop and a vehicle. his wife runs the shop. but people are kind. they do give him money.
i still give him sometimes whenever i have change.

that calmed me down but left me thinking why his family would allow such a deformed man to parade in the city streets.

we did our shopping for the day. dad bought me my fanta and the bun.

he also bought fanta for himself from the supermarket kiosk. we stood by the wall inside the supermarket and consumed our meal in peace. i helped carry the bags of goods my father had purchased for home. we walked back to the lorry station.

we got on the same lorry that had brought us to the city around 2 p.m. my father paid the fare once we arrived at our destination around 4 p.m.

i spent the rest of day talking to my sisters and brothers and cousins about my first city experience. some laughed when i told them how scared i was when i met beggars on the street. some of my brothers and cousins had been to the city already. they knew all about beggars in the city.

my mind was torn apart by the city experience. i could not understand why anyone could choose to leave his or her home village and go begging for food and money from strangers in the city.

i always thought people travelled to the city to work or sell their produce like my father and other people in the village did.

nobody ever went around the village begging for food. my mother would sometimes scold us if we accepted food from neighbors.
she would say that if i got used to accepting food from our neighbors i could end up as beggar.
i never understood the meaning of that statement until now.

i really did not want to end up as a beggar. from that day onwards i would not accept food from any of my friends' parents. if we were playing at one of my friend's home and my friend's mother started cooking food, i would immediately leave for my home. i promised myself i was never going to be a beggar in my life.

Love my village.

in my village.
as i awake at dawn, i hear nature
awakening.
i hear the birds saying their morning
prayers.
i hear the forest waking up to
greet the wind and the sun.

i hear the guinea fowl and the dove
in morning song.
i love nature. i am staying
with nature.

It takes a beer to raise this man.

the man who lived in the village was not ashamed to tell his story of survival in poverty.
he was poor and married.
he lived next door to his parents.
when he got married, he just never moved away to start his own little farm. he liked the local brew we call chibouk so much that he could not do anything productive.
his parents constantly quarreled with him. they tried to get him to stop his drinking and become a real father to his five children. his story in his words:

i call myself a farmer. oh, what a joke!

i have no cattle. i have no goat. i have no chicken.
my hut has a leaky roof. all i do is breed mice and lice.

i am not kidding. go into that hut of mine.
help yourself to mice. if i could sell mice and lice, i would be rich.
i hate some people in this village. i hate my mother.
she yells at me every morning. she tells me i have traded my head for a gourd of beer. yes, i love chibouk. it tastes bitter but is i like it.
my mother tells me i have an empty head. the chibouk fills my empty head. when i go to sleep with my head full of the brew, i don't feel the pain of mosquito and lice bite. as chibouk bubbles in my head the rhythm lulls me to a deep slumber. i snore loudly. my dreams are wonderful. i wish i did not have to

wake up in the morning. i hate the mosquitoes. they disturb my beautiful dreams. sometimes when i wake up my eyes are full of dust. my nose is full of dust. when i blow my nose in the morning mucus mixed with dust shoots out. i hate the pain of lice bite to my head. i don't like living next to my parents. i should move to another village. but i don't have anything to my name. i have to force my wife to go beg for corn meal and salt and sugar and milk every day from my parents.

when my mother is angry with me, she tells me not to step into her yard. she says i stink and i spread lice and mice. she says i am old and i should not go near her hoping to suck milk from her breast. she says i should go consult a witch doctor to cleanse me of my laziness and drinking habit. she says i am

possessed by a ghost of poverty. she
says i will die like a homeless
beggar.
mother's words of wisdom became
true.
the poor lazy man got drunk the last
time and fell asleep in the bushes.
he was eaten by large python.
we miss him for his drunken humor.

Harvest time

fields are brown and the corn is ripe.
water melons and sweet cane have
matured. dry winds prevail with the
chaff.

grasshoppers are fattened and birds
are constipated with grain. with a
sickle and a sac men and women,
boys and girls march and crisscross
the fields in harvest mode.

the squirrels and the quails and
birds are up the trees with full
bellies of grain. they know not how
to till the land nor plant the seed,
yet know how to harvest.

A beautiful morning.

i rise. i awake. the african
summer sun rises from the east.
open your eyes. i do. open your soul.
i do. it is a beautiful morning. a
greenery view with cascading
forest onto the hills west

across the savanna and beyond
there is a velvet mist with a glint and
sparkle as the sun filters in the
morning shadows.
diamonds of morning dew cling
to the tall grass bent over.

i gently close my eyes and open
my soul and let the morning
beauty dissolve. let my night
dreams sublime beyond the
morning blue sky.

breezes of the morning, tenderly
touch my naked soul with an
embrace of tranquility and eternal
peace.

it is not a passing dream.
i love this forest. beautiful forest.
my home that i left behind in africa.

life is a journey.

there!
go my child into the world. it is a vast world. take an adventure. there are many roads. choose wisely. take the road that fits your feet and your heart.
there are many destinations. go to the one that accepts your visa with your face on it.

there are many hotels along the way. choose the one your wallet can afford and your body can rest in with comfort.

there are many temptations along the way. avoid the ones that will overcome you. avoid the ones that will haunt your soul and your body for the rest of your life.

a journey that begins without a plan or without a map will end up in unplanned destination.

Children are victims of war.

in the world of strife, children have
no life. children are born and
blown up by bombs.
no toys. no joy in this world of
terror. hungry and starved right
from the womb.
mothers' toil takes its toll.
trodden upon and soiled, mothers
grieve. death fills the graves.

mindless and endless wars of death
continue unabated.
senseless mind set to conquer the
other race, the other tribe, the other
religion to submit to the one with a
superior weapon of death.

there is no justification for these
hopeless massacres of innocent
children and women and men.

i call on you all whose judgment is
forcefully clear and unbiased. cry
out loud to the sky for these
murderous wars to stop.
stop this insanity. stop.........

Death in the villages and slums.

in the villages of africa, children are
born in mud houses
amidst flies and deadly mosquitoes,
hunger and poverty.
children are born. others grow.
others go to school.

children die. hunger kills. malaria
kills.
disease maims. tears drop. tears dry.
graves open. children are buried.
mothers die. fathers die. aids kills.

death lingers on. marking its
territory on grave mounds
under the tree shadows. no one
has been able to stop its march.

everyone is afraid as the
night approaches.
everyday death claims
innocent lives.

lives unfulfilled.
prematurely obliterated.
where is the power and the will to
stop this death march?

Love is here to stay.

when love arrives, roses grow
when love descends tulips flower
when love settles all flowers bloom.

Let the sun shine in you.

after the fog has dissipated from the
valleys of your soul
after the dark cloud has passed by in
your life
the sun will brighten the path
of your life and your soul.

My gift to be born.

life,
this is a precious gift given to us.
it should not be taken away
from anyone prematurely.
it should be nurtured to the fullest.
life is what shapes and controls
our physical body.
the body should be nourished fully.
the being, the body, the mind, the
soul makeup the pillars of life

together these pillars make
us complete humans.
we are born as complete humans
with full rights.

no other human being should hate,
spit at, shoot or discriminate
against another human.

no other human has the right
to dominate, enslave, rob or
maim another human.

the rights, capabilities, physical and
mental abilities bestowed upon us at
creation, no other human of any
race shall or can or may yank it
from you.

life is precious. it is yours. it
is sanctified.
all human race, the collective human
race has to adhere to this tenet.

Light up your heart.

the being in you awakens when
the sun rises
the heavy blanket of darkness
recedes into the shadows of
the forest.
if you let the darkness in your heart
and soul escape into the shadows

the light of the sun will come
into you.
once the light is inside you, shut all
the windows to your heart and
soul. never let the light escape.

then you become the light to those
around you and to all those who
remain under the dark blanket.

you feel tears welling up in you as
the sun finds its depth in you. open

up and let the tears flow out of you. that is the way darkness dissolves out of your soul. feel the beginning of the healing process.

as the light settles inside the heart and burns away the dark clouds in you, the healing of the mind, soul and body begins.

Now that I am old.

now that i am old, i have taken to
writing my memories down. i am
unable to write to memory.
i am no longer able to
memorize words or names.
i have trouble calling my children
by their right names.
sometimes i have to call up all the
names of my children. it takes a
while to settle on the right name.

i have trouble recalling names of
people i work with. situations always
arise when a co-worker greets me by
my name. in that instant their name
vanishes from my lips and gets stuck
at the bottom of my memory.

so, i just respond to the greeting
with a loud enthusiastic hello and
how are you today? and fill up

the conversation with weather news etc.

that loud enthusiastic response masks my confused state of mind. failing to recall the name of someone i have spent many years with makes me feel ridiculous and stupid.

then i spend the rest of the day trying to dig up the name of that person out of the bottom of my memory. i lose my concentration on my days task. when my mind cannot dig up the name, eventually i have to sneak around and ask people who are not friends with the person whose name i cannot recall. i cannot ask the friends for they may tell the person about my memory problem.

but misfortune strikes. word spreads quickly. someone has leaked my secret. i know this because every time i meet one of my co-workers,

they tell me their name first and
then greet me.
word has gone wild around: he
is losing his marbles!!

Getting old.

counting seasons and moons
has made me weary and old. i
have now lost count.
and now i forget to count.
i am not growing up any more.

i am growing down. i keep my eyes
focused on this narrow path leading
to the end of life.
since i lost count of the moons
and seasons
my age is now measured by
strength and weakness,
aches and pains in my body.

I miss the sun.

i miss eating the grape of the sun
i miss bathing in the warm rain
from the sun
i miss the full love of the sun's ocean
that fills the heavenly sky.
when i am immersed in the
deep side the of the sun's ocean
my crystallized pain dissipates
slowly to the ocean floor of my heart
and i can feel that motion.

Colorblind.

our love to explore has kept us
tied together.
i am black and she is white.
in the beginning of our love we
rubbed skins against each other.
nothing changed. she remained
white. i remained black.

on the following days of love, i fed
her black beans. and she fed me
white milk. nothing changed. she
remained white. i remained black.

weeks later she gave me a bath
mixed with her blood. i gave her a
bath with my saliva.
nothing changed. she remained
white. i remained black.

on many nights of our love we
shared the nights in total darkness.

from the touch she could not tell the
color of my skin and nor could i tell
the color of her skin. all body parts
felt good. when day break came she
was still white and i was still black.
after many moons of love, i went to
tell my uncle about my love with a
white woman. she went to tell her
priest about her love with a black
man.

my uncle gave me love portion to
drink and told me to share it with
her. she returned with a shiny
ring as advised by her priest.
i gave her the love portion to drink.
she gave me the shinning ring.

after we drank the love portion,
we both went blind. we became
colorblind. ever since, we have

remained colorblind and
racially free. we are still bound
by the shinning ring of love.

Village celebrations.

a lonely drummer, deep in the
hills, strums a drum.
the sound of the drum
reverberates over the hills.
you hear the strong sound as the
wind vibrates throughout the forest
of the land.

you see the birds in the air over the
african forest as they fly and sore
up beyond into the blue sky.

you see women and men of the land
dressed in colors of the butterfly and
the leopard dancing and marching
in rhythm into the open wind-swept
dance arena. a song of jubilation
pierces the wind and you know the
celebrations have just began.

the blowing wind is full of a rich
smell of the people's brew, chibuku.
fermentation of the brew has
completed the seven-day bubbling
period.
the rich aroma of the bubbly brew is
truly inviting to the spirit of the
land.
take a gourd full of chibuku. this is
a drink of the land

from all the sound rhythms and
vibrations emanating from four
corners of the dance arena, you
know the festival has just began. the
song of kalindula and the rhythm of
the drum, in high note, will lift you
off the ground and throw you into
the dance arena. the gyrating
buttocks of the young women in the
middle of the dance arena
mesmerizes. the dead rise to their
feet. you know the dance festival has
gone into high gear.

we gather to celebrate, to bathe in joyous song, to soak our souls in the music of our history of oneness, of bravery, of kindness and of love.

this is also the festival where broken hearts are mended, wounded bodies are healed and chained souls are liberated. let your heart and soul celebrate.

Standing in the valley.

i stand here in the valley facing the
great mountain. clouds slowly ascend
to the lofty sky, silently flying away
over the mountain. a metallic grey
mist freely floats above.
the majestic hand of creation
looms upon the mountain.

below the mountain there is a
crater, the footstep of the creator.
a giant boulder lies motionless. this
was the backrest for the creator
here in the dense valley.
when i arrive here at the base, in the
valley, of the great mountain
i stand here in great owe, in
wonderment. i open up and let my
eyes, my mind and my soul sore
high up over the dense valley unto

the mountain top and get filled
with power and beauty of creation.
i raise my hands and feel the power
and breeze. peace and tranquility
hug me gently as my soul waltzes
over the great mountain. it is a
wonderful view.

Love nature

i wake up on a bright morning,
walking on a shaded path, lofty
branches sway gently, leaves
descend gently to ground. blooming
petals of flowers on twisted vines
shine my path.

shadows of the tall forest lie
in silence.
the green grass of summer waves at
me in silence.

some other mornings, the forest is
not that quiet. it is filled with
soothing sounds of the dove, the
blue bird and the guinea fowl and
a myriad of insects as they
welcome me to the beautiful forest.

i love the sounds of nature.

as i walk towards the river, my lungs open up and inhale the soothing and calming fresh air of the forest. i feel refreshed and green inside me. i love the taste of nature.

Born free in this jungle.

you are born in this jungle.
you belong to this jungle.
you are born free in this jungle.
there are types of people in this
jungle we live in:
don't let the mosquito types or
the tsetse fly types

or the horsefly types or the
snake types
of this jungle scare you or take a bite
on your freedom of existence.

even if you encounter the lion types
of this jungle, you just have to let
the elephant in you raise its giant
trunk. scream.
let everyone know you belong to this
jungle.

The little secrets that bug you.

there is a little dirt pig in you
leading you
into dirtier corners of the
heart's conversation.
when this conversation comes to
an end,
write the story of the conversation.

tell your friend about it. it's not
worth your life to be burdened by
this dirty conversation. the little
dirty secrets will clog up your heart.
let them go.

tell someone you trust.

Evil thought.

it hurts a little. it burns
and sometimes hates.
you know there is an evil little
fire that churns in your belly.
it hurts others when the little evil
fire flares up in you.

why not gather all your hatred,
your evil thoughts, your unkind
words, your racist slurs, your
insults and your demeaning
remarks; overflowing in your belly
and set them on fire?

take the leftover ashes and
spread them over in your garden
and let roses grow instead!

Afraid of fear.

fear grips you with
strengthened violence.
your physical body is paralyzed.
you know from the trembles of
your hand,
your speech is strangled. you
are left in state of shock

unable to activate the rest of your
senses to the stimuli they receive.
fear wraps you tightly from your
inner being to the outer layer of you.
it wraps you in a tight bind.

your breathing comes in short
gasps. but when you confront fear
with a gentle soul
slightly nudging and pulling down
the wrap around

and unwrapping the grip of fear
with confidence of your strengths
it will certainly dissolve and
evaporate with your breath.
whatever fears you might
have; courage will set you free.

Life never dies.

when i die, lay my body in the grave. let my body rot and let the soil eat it away.
let me rot. let me return to dust. let my flesh return to earth.
let it become part of the earth. let the roots of the trees find my blood filled with iron and milk. let the trees grow in my blood.

when you come to the grave and find trees and grass and flowers growing then you know i am still alive. give the tree and the grass and the flowers a big hug. call the trees by my name. i will answer by swaying in the wind and with a waltz.

when your body dies and buried,
life continues.

your life remains alive to tell

the story of your past journey.

Closer to the mother.

while you were a baby, still in
the mother womb,
only your mother could hear you
playing or crying or laughing.
only your mother could hear the first
conversations you had.

only your mother knows baby
secrets.
now that your grown don't hide
your secret from her.
you're closest to your
mother's heart.

My Life battles.

i don't have words and strength left
to tell you about my battles of life. i
will let my inner scars tell you the
battles of my life.
and i want to let you in on my
small secret:
i have buried my failures under
the mountain that i have
successfully climbed: mount life.

Touched by my whistling

one morning i stopped at a convenience store to buy my morning coffee. i went to the self-serve coffee station. i stood next to a white woman.
i do like to make a low whistling sound. i do this unconsciously. i just blow air through between my lips and a light whistling sound comes out.

that morning i was whistling, unconsciously, while i mixed my coffee contents. i was unaware that the woman standing next to me was stealing glances at me. when i was ready to go to pay for my coffee the woman turned and faced me with tears and a smile on her face.

she had tears in her eyes. "i am sorry to interrupt your morning, but i have to tell you that your whistling made me tear up." she picked up a paper towel and wiped her tears.

i couldn't believe my ears. i couldn't believe what she was telling me. she continued her speech: "*your whistling sounded exactly like my late dad's. when i heard your whistling, i thought my mind was playing games. but when i stole a glance at you, luckily you didn't catch me, i was certain it was you and not dad's ghost that i had heard whistling.*"

we stood there facing each other like strangers who had found love on a blind date. her tears were bubbling out of her blue eyes and her smile was still genuine on her lips. i didn't fall in love with her but i was overcome by her sincerity. “i am sorry for your loss,” i said stretching my arms to give her a morning hug. she gave me a tight hug and thanked me profusely. “this was most wonderful morning experience since my dad passed away. i am thankful for this encounter,” she said and quickly picked up her coffee container and went to pay for her coffee.

we never exchanged names or phone numbers. i lingered a little longer in the store and finally went up to the cashier to pay for my coffee. the cashier waved me to go without paying and handed me a donut.
i went out to my car and sat down for a while. i felt the presence of a dad and her daughter having quiet morning coffee.

my heart and soul were filled with joy. i enjoyed my coffee in their presence.

Remember these words.

it is not the high mountain that
threatens, it is the climb to the top of
the mountain that i am afraid of.
it is not lack of the light that i
am afraid of; it is not knowing
what lurks in the dark.

it is not the light from the fire that i
am afraid of, it is the heat from the
fire that poses danger.

it is not the roar of the lion that
scares me, it what the killer bite the
lion can do to you.
it is not the buzzing sound of the
bees that scares me, it is the sting of
the bee.

it is not the color or the appearance
or gender or size of the person that

scares me, it is the racial slurs, evil looks, superiority posturing from these kinds of people that i am afraid of.

Wisdom for you.

wisdom,
wise words,
good advice passed on from the
lips of our elders
and those who have acquired
knowledge over the years
has density. it sinks and stays inside
your heart.

The light of your life.

each person touched by your
good deeds,
by your generosity,
by your smiles,
by your love
by the work you do,
by the words of wisdom, you
give, by your kindness, by your
humility,
by all positive deeds from your heart
becomes part of your own universe.

each of these people becomes the
shining star in that universe. when
you lay down, or sit down under the
shadows of your life, or when you
are gone out of this world, the stars
in that universe will shine on. the
light of your life will shine on forever
in that universe.

By the sea.

by the seashore
i stand here and listen to the waves.
by the seashore
waves rise in me
waves die in me.

by the seashore
the storm rises in me
the storm dies within.
by the sea shore

sea gulls dive into the murky
waters of my soul
seagulls fish out dead thoughts out
of my mind.

by the seashore
the wind blows away all my sorrows.
by the seashore

the blue water cleanses my heart,
my soul and mind. it makes me
sparkle with youthful life.

www.ingramcontent.com/pod-product-compliance
Lightning Source LLC
Chambersburg PA
CBHW030934060726
47591CB00005B/1789

* 9 7 8 1 9 9 9 2 1 0 5 0 2 *